MANNERS MATTER!

Written by Veronica Zysk   **Introduction by Temple Grandin**

Temple Talks to Kids Series: MANNERS MATTER!

All marketing and publishing rights guaranteed to and reserved by:

FUTURE HORIZONS INC.

721 W. Abram St. Arlington, TX 76013

Toll-free: 800·489·0727 | Fax: 817·277·2270

www.FHautism.com | info@FHautism.com

Text and illustrations © 2018 Veronica Zysk

All rights reserved.

Printed in Canada.

No part of this product may be reproduced in any manner whatsoever without written permission of Future Horizons, except in the case of brief quotations embodied in reviews.

ISBN: 9781941765593

Dedication

To the child spirit in all of us,
where we find a world of magic and possibilities
in a jar of fireflies

A Personal Note to Kids from Temple Grandin

As a child of the 1950s, manners were taught to all children. The social rules around manners were the same at my house as they were at my friends' houses. When I went to other homes to play with my friends, the other mothers corrected all the children. Teaching children good manners was considered important, and everyone pitched in.

The structured ways that manners were taught in the 1950s and the general expectation that *all* kids would learn manners helped many children who were socially awkward to adapt. I can think of several college friends and teachers who were probably Asperger's with no speech delay. Having good manners helped them keep and hold jobs. Their manners made socializing easier. People would overlook some of their quirkiness because they functioned within the social rules of the time.

Be true to yourself. You are different, but not less. It is acceptable to be eccentric. Eccentric and unique is fine, but being rude, unkind, or not knowing how to interact with others at the basic level of "please," "thank you," or "excuse me" is *never* acceptable. Manners help people exist together and get along with each other. They will open doors that will give you a chance to express yourself, be yourself, and achieve your goals and dreams. I know from experience that this is possible. Just keep learning and trying!

— Temple Grandin
Professor of Animal Science
Colorado State University

About Temple Grandin

Temple Grandin is world famous for many things! She can think in pictures—that means she can see pictures in her mind that represent her thoughts and ideas, sort of like the drawings in this book show the ideas we're talking about.

Isn't that amazing?

Temple grew up in Colorado, attended public school, graduated from college, and then started working with companies who make big corrals for cows and other types of livestock. She was very, very talented at drawing blueprints for these corrals. Month by month, and year by year, Temple got better and better at her job. Now she works with companies all over the world!

Animals have a special place in Temple's heart. *Maybe they do in your heart, too?*

Temple writes books and speaks to people around the world about her work, and also about growing up and being a person with autism. *Maybe you know someone with autism?*

Now Temple and her friend Veronica are writing a series of books especially for kids, kids just like you! They want to tell you stories of what it was like for Temple as she was growing up and some things Temple learned that can help you too.

Isn't that great? Let's say "Thank you, Temple! Thank you, Veronica!"

... because after all, manners matter!

Hi, my name is Temple Grandin.
What's yours?

I live in Colorado.
Which state do you live in?

I have reddish-brown hair that gets curly when it rains.
What color is your hair?

I like to dress in western clothes and cowboy boots.
What are your favorite clothes to wear?

And ... I have autism,
which means my brain works a little differently
than most people's brains.

Every person is unique.
Some things may be the same about us
and some things may be different ... and that's okay.

When I was young, around your age,
I really, really, really liked to spend my time
doing my favorite things,
like painting pictures or building things.

My autism brain was like a super fast mini-computer
in my head. My thinking was in pictures,
and that made it easier for me to learn some things.

But my autism also made some things
not so easy for me to learn.
Some things just didn't make sense,
or they didn't seem all that important to me.

Especially how to behave around other people.
I called it "social stuff."

My mother and teachers used to tell me I needed to learn how to talk and act around other people:

To say "please" and "thank you."
How to introduce myself and shake hands
How to behave in public.
How to get along with other kids.
How to act at the dinner table or in a restaurant.

She called all this social stuff ... MANNERS.
In our house, manners were the rules!

All kids were expected to learn these things, not just me.
And my autism didn't matter ... I still needed
to learn manners.

When I was young, I didn't think manners were all that interesting to learn—
but I was expected I learn them!
If I didn't, there were consequences,
like not being able to watch my favorite shows on TV.

I needed lots and LOTS of reminders about
using my manners!
I kept trying … and practicing …
(and making mistakes sometimes).

After a while it got easier and I started using them
on my own. And you know what?

As I got older and went from elementary school to middle school, and then graduated from college and became an adult, manners really helped me.

Hmm … I guess manners are a good thing
if I want to learn how to be around other people!

In this book, I want to tell you about some of the manners
I learned so you can learn more about them, too!

Manners are social rules people follow so everyone can get
along. Manners show others you are kind and sensitive to
their feelings.

Manners are things you say (or don't say)
and sometimes things you do (or don't do).

It doesn't always feel right or good,
but here's what I learned:
Other people judge you based on what you say and do.

Most of the time, using good manners is good
no matter where you are or who you are with.
It's called "being polite."

Some manners you can use anyplace, anytime, and with all kinds of people. Some manners, like table manners, are used only in certain situations.

Let's start by talking about the "always manners." These are manners everyone should know about and everyone should use!

Say "please" when asking for something
Say "thank you" or "thanks"
when something is offered or given to you.

Say "no, thank you" when you don't want what someone is offering you.

If you do something wrong, or that might have hurt someone else's feelings, say "I'm sorry."

18

Say "excuse me" if you have to move your body around someone else, or if you need to interrupt people who are talking.

If someone asks you a question, it's good manners to answer it politely. And you are even more polite if you ask the person a question in return!

We all like to be acknowledged. That means we show others we are listening to them and we care about them. It makes everyone feel good!

When I was just learning about manners,
I would sometimes forget to use them.

If I forgot or I did something wrong, Mother was helpful.
She knew I was trying my best,
so she never scolded me or yelled
or told me what I was doing wrong.
Instead, she would always remind me of what to do!

Manners can take a lot of practice to learn!
The good thing is you use them everyday
in all different situations,
so there are LOTS and LOTS of chances to practice!

Some manners are "everyday manners,"
but they're used only at certain times and
in certain situations.

For example, there are a LOT of special manners about
how to behave when you're eating!
They're called "table manners."

You can use these manners at breakfast, lunch,
and dinner—
when you're at your house,
when you're eating at a friend's house,
and when you're at a restaurant.

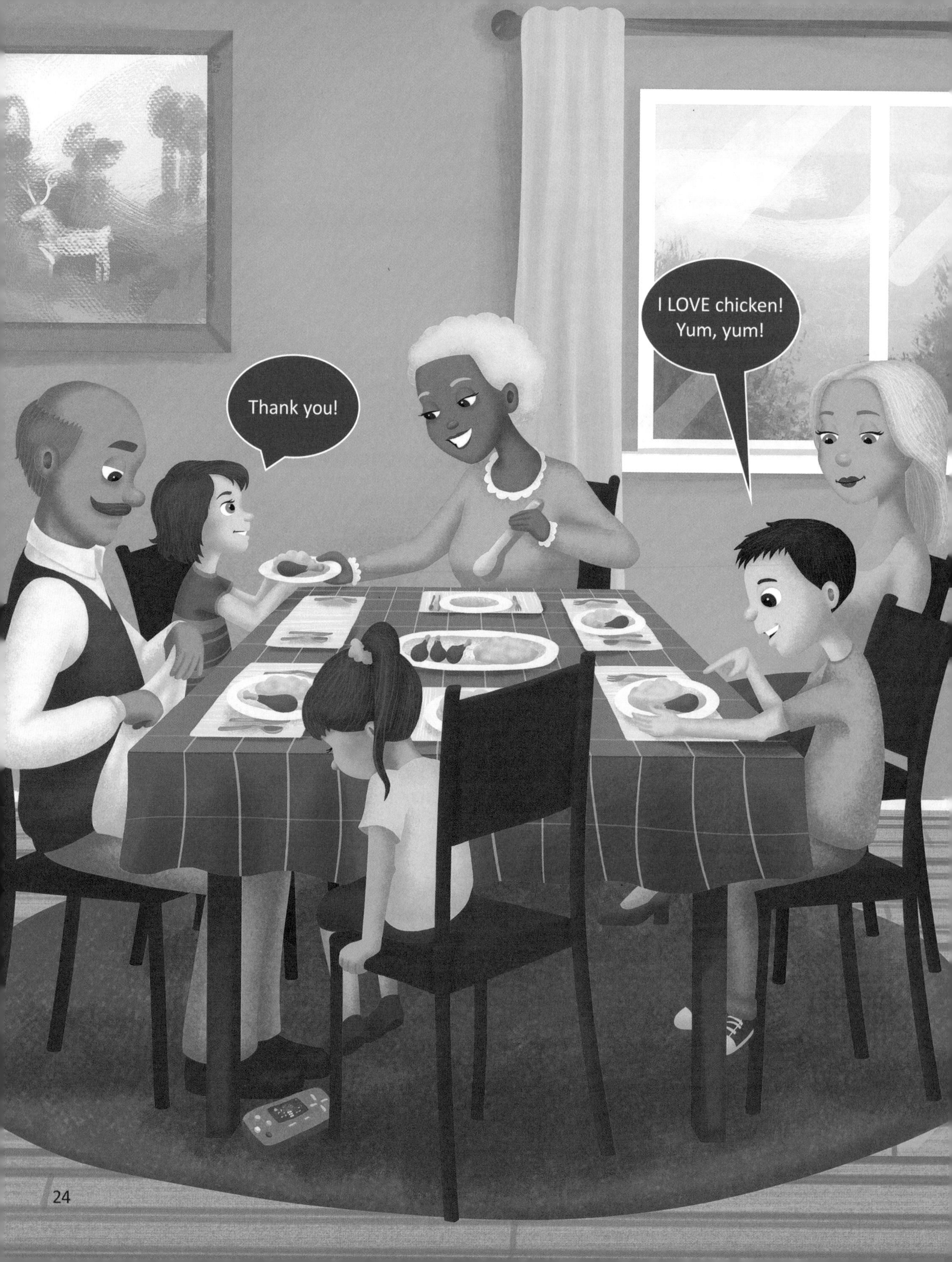
Thank you!
I LOVE chicken!
Yum, yum!

Here are some everyday table manners I learned
about that will help you, too!

Wash your hands before eating.
Put your napkin in your lap when you sit down.
Wait until everyone else has their food before
you start eating.

Talk quietly to others at the table.
Stay seated during the meal.

Leave your cell phone, tablet,
or video games in another room.
(I know, this can be a hard one to learn!)

Use your fork, spoon, and knife unless you're eating "finger food" like pizza, a sandwich, a hot dog in a bun, or potato chips.

Chew your food with your mouth closed.
Finish chewing your food before talking.

Ask for something you need if it's out of reach.
Pass food to others to the right of you.
Use your napkin to wipe your mouth.

If grown-ups are talking, wait until they finish before saying something.

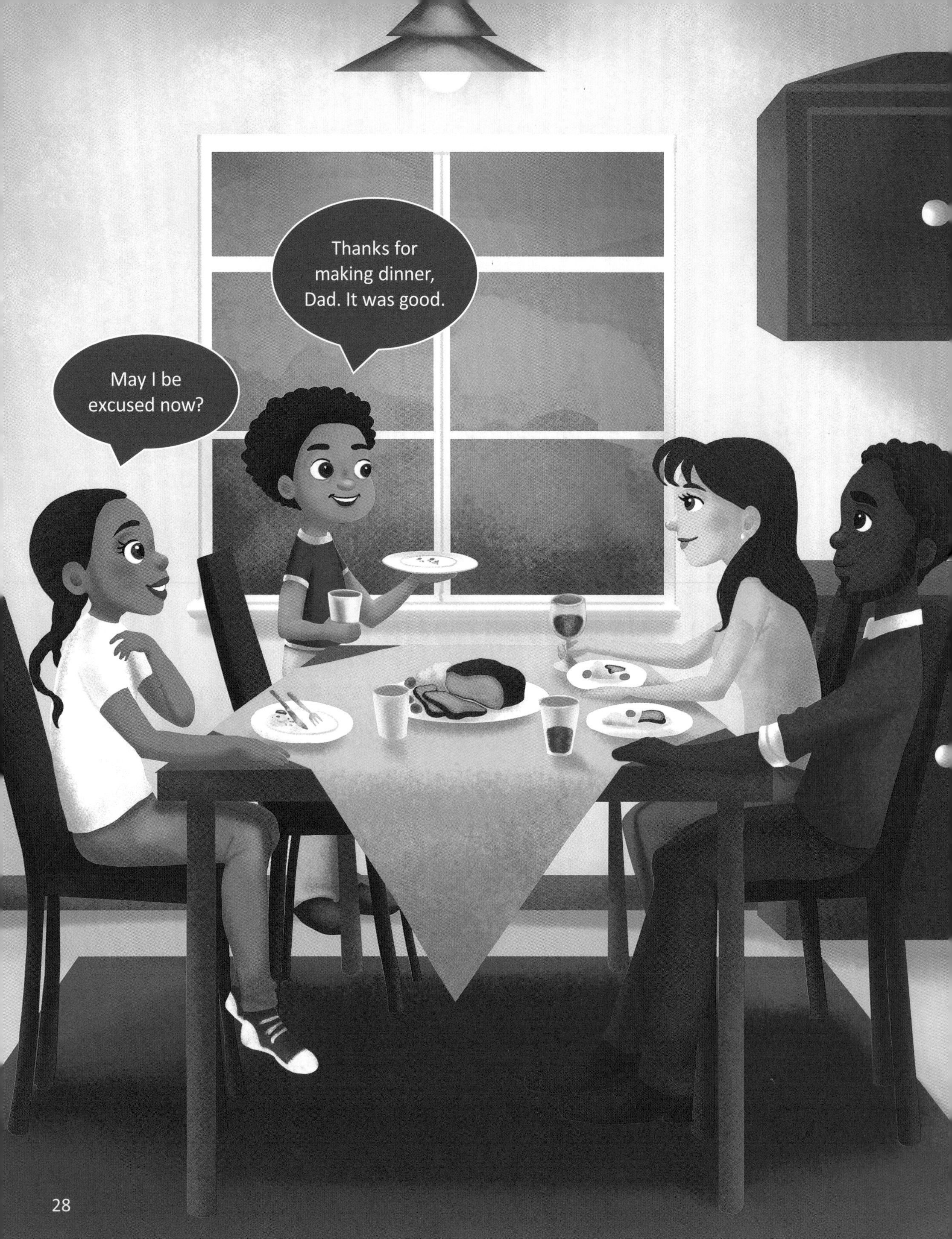
May I be excused now?
Thanks for making dinner, Dad. It was good.

There are some table manners to use
when you're done eating, too!

Put your knife and fork in the four o'clock position—
this tells others you're done eating.

Ask to be excused when you've finished eating.

When you're leaving the table: push in your chair,
pick up your plate, utensils, and glass,
and take them into the kitchen.

Before leaving the table, say "thank you"
to the person who cooked the food.

When I was growing up, we always had dinner
at the dining room table.
Sometimes I would forget one of the table rules.
Sometimes my mistake was a BIG mistake!

Even then, Mother was cool and calm.
She simply told me what I should be doing
instead of what I was doing wrong.

One time we had roast beef, mashed potatoes,
and peas for dinner. I was really hungry and put a BIG
forkful of everything in my mouth at the same time.

Just then, my sister asked me about my horseback riding
lesson. I was so excited to tell her,
I forgot my table manners.
I started talking with my mouth full of food!

Uh oh!

32

I learned a lot of other manners
while playing board games with my sister or other kids,
and when we were shopping at a store (like the grocery
store) or going out for ice cream.

Manners help us remember to be nice to other people,
to try to get along, and not do things that may hurt
their feelings.

Some other manners to remember include:
Keep unkind or mean thoughts to yourself,
especially about other people's physical characteristics.

Share your toys and games when you're playing with others.
Remember that everyone wants to have a turn during play.

Knock first on closed doors before entering.

CAFETERIA
Where are her manners?
I'm going to lap up my ice cream like a dog. The kids are going to think this is really funny!
Ugh, gross!
Weird!
Yuck!

So why are manners so important?

When we have good manners and are polite to others,
we make a good impression on other people.

That means people around us will have
good thoughts about us.
When they have good thoughts about us, they will want
to be around us, play with us, and spend time with us.

But the opposite is true, too!
When we don't have good manners and we're not polite
to others, people may have unkind, weird, or creepy
thoughts about us.

That can make them feel nervous or uncomfortable.

They may not want to spend time with us, play with us,
or be friends with us.

That's not good!

The thoughts people have about us are powerful!

When other people have good thoughts about us, it means
we have more chances to be around others.
That helps us make friends, work in groups at school,
and have fun playing with others.

When we get older, having good manners helps us
get through school, go on to college (if we want to),
find jobs, be team members, and have friends!

I'm glad the adults in my life took the time
to teach me manners.
It took practice and more practice
(and sometimes even more practice!)
and I didn't always get them right.

But I kept trying ... and I'm glad I did!

20 Tips for Parents & Caregivers of Children with ASD

(For all parents, too!)

Manners are the social behaviors that help us get along with others within our culture and society. No matter where we call home, the basic social niceties of "please," "thank you," or "excuse me" are a universal language.

Like it or not, other people judge our behaviors. They observe what we're saying or doing and immediately have thoughts and feelings about us. In turn, these thoughts and feelings determine how they act in response to us. If they have positive thoughts, they view us as nice or respectful and will want to continue to be around us. If they have negative thoughts or uncomfortable feelings, they may think we're odd, rude, or uncaring. Who wants to be around someone who makes us feel that way?

In her writings and face-to-face presentations, Temple repeatedly stresses one thing: *autism is not an excuse for bad behavior*. It's undeniable that a child's autism spectrum disorder (ASD) may mean that, as adults, we need to think harder and be more creative about how we teach good manners to our spectrum kids. Their brains don't come equipped with the same "social genes" as their neurotypical peers. They need to be taught directly and concretely (and through a lot more practice) what other kids seem to learn through watching what's happening around them, or with some minor instruction and correction by adults.

As a direct result of how their brains function and process social information, kids with ASD deal with more than their share of challenges. Sensory issues complicate their lives even further. As parents and caregivers, we are their most ardent teachers, and others—especially their peers—are their most ardent critics. Toss aside even the slightest notion that their ASD gives them some sort of social "pass," or that others will make allowances for their unsocial behaviors and lack of manners. That's just not the reality of everyday life, especially as they grow up and peers become less forgiving and adults expect them to "know better by now."

Good manners help ASD kids gain entry to the social world. Think of them as their gateway to social interaction with others. Our spectrum kids need so much more practice to learn social skills, and that means interacting with others. Good manners open the door and provide them with opportunities to engage, learn, and grow, so that even when our kids make the inevitable social blunders, others will give them a second chance (or a third or fourth).

In putting this book together, Temple stressed several things adults in her life did and that helped her learn good manners.

1. ***Know your child!*** Know your child's preferred learning style, as well as their level of social understanding and perspective-taking. Being able to understand social cause and effect—the "why" behind manners—is dependent on being able to take another person's perspective.

2. ***Model the good manners*** you are trying to teach your child. It's confusing at best for a child to be taught to say "please" or "no, thank you" when parents or caregivers are not demonstrating these behaviors themselves.

3. ***Use video modeling and media as tools!*** Enlist the help of your child and siblings to act out good manners while you video record them. Kids love watching themselves later. Point out good manners while watching movies, TV shows, and favorite videos. Even animated characters can have good manners!

4. ***Define the manner in a way that is meaningful*** for the child. Some kids respond better to making manners part of the "social rules" than long-winded verbal explanations about why it's important to others, or their futures.

5. ***Consider using visuals and nonverbal prompts*** so the child can be successful in learning to use manners independently. Why? If you always use a verbal cue such as "say no, thank you," your child may come to rely on your prompt to figure out what to do. No prompt, no good manners. Add in visuals and nonverbal cues so you can fade out the verbal prompt and the child can move toward independence.

6. ***Set expectations and define consequences.*** It's pointless to try to teach manners, or any social behavior, without expectations and consequences.

7. ***No surprises!*** Be sure you've explained expectations and consequences ahead of time to the child, and that they fit the developmental age and processing ability of the child.

8. ***Be sensory savvy.*** Do understand when sensory challenges are preventing your child from showing good manners you know they have learned and can demonstrate. Maybe the room is just too busy, too noisy, and there's too much sensory stimuli for them to remember how to introduce themselves at that moment. Adjust expectations and consequences accordingly.

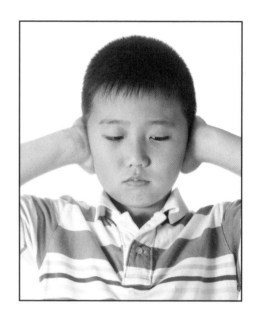

9. Parents and caregivers: ***be consistent in your behavior***—apart and together! If your expectations waver from one day to the next, if mom holds one perspective toward manners and dad holds another, or you enforce consequences on a "sometimes" basis, your child's behavior will be, at best, "sometimes" too. That's a frustrating experience for all of you!

10. ***Good manners are a habit;*** they are skills we learn! And learning them is all about repetition. Use the hundreds of natural experiences in a day to teach in the moment and help your child learn good manners.

11. ***Do correct, but keep it positive.*** Temple mentioned her mother never—and she stressed never—told her "don't do xyz," or asked her something like, "What are you forgetting to say/do?" ***She always told her what to do in the situation, what was the right behavior.*** Kids with ASD can't figure this out on their own when you say "don't do that," so tell them what to do instead!

12. When offering correction, ***first get your child's attention.*** Then look at your child, perhaps get down at the child's level, and say what you plan to say. If you don't have your child's attention, you're not teaching and they're not learning.

13. ***Keep your language simple*** and try to use the same or similar instructional language consistently.

14. ***Keep calm,*** talk in a calm voice, and keep your feelings in check.

15. ***Provide lots of positive reinforcement,*** even for trying and when they may not get things quite right.

16. ***Figure out what motivates your child*** to learn good manners. Some kids with classic autism may respond better to a token reward system where they earn stars or points toward some special treat. Kids with Asperger's or ASD Level 1 may be sensitive to the fact that their behaviors  affect others around them in unfavorable ways. Their desire to have friends or be accepted by their peers may be motivating to the point that a verbal "good job" or "Aunt Frankie mentioned how polite you were to her" is reinforcement enough.

17. And about those rewards: *it should always be about earning* and not about losing rewards. Maybe the reward is earning fifteen more minutes of computer time, rather than docking the child fifteen minutes. Check your language in how you're talking to your child when mishaps occur. The consequence is that they're not earning anything at that time, rather than they're losing out. Make sense? Losing is not motivating at all!

18. *Look for ways to make manners something fun* to learn! You can find games for teaching good manners on the Internet.

19. *Enlist the support of family and friends.* Talk to aunts and uncles, grandparents, babysitters, and friends to join you in reinforcing the manners you're teaching. It benefits all kids, not just your own, and reminds adults that manners matter, too!

20. *Be patient.* Having good manners is a lifelong learning experience. Go slowly, introduce new social skills one-by-one, and teach manners according to your child's learning abilities.